W9-DAF-163

Snake in the Strawberries

Snake in the Strawberries

SELECTED POEMS BY
J A M E S   H E A R S T

IOWA STATE UNIVERSITY PRESS / AMES

1 9 7 9

The publisher and author acknowledge permission to reprint poems that have ap-
peared in the following publications: "Bereaved," *American Scholar;* "Women Shear-
ing Men," *Canadian Forum;* "The Chipmunk and I," *Chicago Tribune Magazine;*
"The Will to Possess," *Chowder Review;* "Born Each Morning," *Colorado Quarterly;*
"Cock Pheasant," *Crazy Horse;* "Veteran's Day," *Des Moines Register and Tribune;*
"A Disowner," "No More Chores," *Event;* "Alive and Well," "Flight and Return,"
"Growing Up," "Hostility to Order," "Lock the Door," "Same Thing but Dif-
ferent," "Vacation in Colorado," "The Way It Is," "Whatever Happened," "Who?
Who?" *Great Lakes Review;* "Games Are Never Free," *Iowa Arts Council Newsletter;*
"Routine Keeps Me," *KPFA Folio;* "End of the Game," *Lake Superior Review;* "It
Never Went Away," "Words that Smell Bad," *New River Review;* "The Inevitable
Words like Signposts,"*Ohio Review;* "The Oracle," *Poetry;* "Resort to Calm," *Prairie
Schooner;* "Cleaning the Barn," *Small Farm;* "Mother," *South Dakota Review;*
"Dogma," *Virginia Quarterly Review;* "Father," "Forked Road," "Thought of
Bluebells," *Wascana Review;* "The Enemy," "Ute Cemetery," *Westerly Review;*
"Dragon Lesson," "Eighty Birthdays," "End of April," "Not Born Again," *Yankee
Magazine.* Prior publication of the following is also acknowledged: "Here and There,"
Cloud Marauder; "Auction," *Fiction;* "Sharers," *Ladies Home Journal;* "View by
View," *New York Times;* "Out of Season," *Pebble.* We also acknowledge the follow-
ing: "Calendar's Mischief," "A Testament,", reprinted with permission of *America.*
All rights reserved. Copyright 1977 by America Press, Inc., 106 West 56th St., New
York, N.Y. 10019. "Revelation," *Christian Science Monitor,* July 10, 1973. Reprinted
by permission from *The Christian Science Monitor.* © 1973 The Christian Science
Publishing Society. All rights reserved.

© 1979, The Iowa State University Press
All rights reserved

Composed and printed by
The Iowa State University Press
Ames, Iowa 50010

No part of this publication may be reproduced, stored in a retrieval system, or trans-
mitted in any form or by any means—electronic, mechanical, photocopying, recording,
or otherwise—without the prior written permission of the publisher.

First edition, 1979

Library of Congress Cataloging in Publication Data

Hearst, James, 1900–
    Snake in the strawberries.

    I. Title.
PS3515.E146S58   811'.5'2   78–15567
ISBN 0-8138-0765-4

Dedication

to our hired girls and hired men,
to neighbors both country and town,
to students who braved my classes,
to nurses and doctors who helped me,
(and, of course, to family and friends).

Contents

Foreword

You will be rewarded if you read these poems written by Jim Hearst. You will be amused by some, for Jim has a great sense of humor. You will enjoy others, for Jim is a great storyteller. Some will upset you, for Jim does not always deal in sweetness and light.

But more than any of this you will be fascinated by the different angles of human experience into which Jim digs. He writes with a language and imagery that common people can understand. At the same time he expresses a universality and insight into the human condition that is characteristic of all the best poetry.

Jim has mastered the poetic devices. You will not only understand what he says but you will like the rhythms of the words he uses. Poetry must sound just right when it is read aloud; Jim's writing accomplishes this.

If you have farm connections, you will doubly enjoy these selections because Jim uses authentic imagery and idiom that only a real farmer knows. But these are not strictly farm poems. They are about all aspects of life and the problems that people face. The "people" side of farmers and others receives the real emphasis.

I have known Jim as a farmer, as a teacher, and as a man. The more I have been associated with him, the more I have appreciated his understanding and compassion and courage. He is not only "authentic" in his use of farm imagery but he is also completely authentic as a human being. I feel when I read his poems that I am getting the real thing. When you read them, I hope you will think so too.

Donald E. Fish

Preface

   I was born and raised on a farm, and worked on the family farm
the first part of my life. The need for expression seemed never quite
satisfied by the work in barn and field. So I tried in my spare time to
translate farm life into poetry. I did not think of myself as a poet but
rather as a man who attempts to make poems. I had the farmer's
calloused hands, wished for a perceptive mind, and hoped for a loving
heart. I knew the ways of farm animals, read weather signs, waited on
the change of seasons, and sweated to sow and harvest crops.

   When I traded the tractor's seat for the professor's chair, I tried to
persuade my students to open their minds to new experiences of learn-
ing. We followed, my students and I, both strange and familiar roads
leading to the discovery of what values literature brought to our lives. I
encouraged the young women and young men to enter their future
with confidence in the firm ground under their feet, and with curiosity
to see what lay beyond the next step.

   I was never sure where the poems came from. Paul Valery, the
French poet, said, "God gives you the first line, you work out the rest
yourself." I found that something is given, a feeling, idea, image,
rhythm; and as one bone might suggest the skeleton, a whole pattern
emerged from this first small discovery. I tried to learn the pattern of
words called poetry. Sometimes the true shape would not form, and a
distorted figure appeared. The hillside of my intentions was filled with
abandoned efforts. But when pressure and control forced the related
pieces into place and the final line locked them in, the truth was there.
I wanted the poem to wear on its face an expression of this truth,
revelation, insight, whatever you wish to call the meaning. The reader
should recognize it as the face of a friend suddenly remembered. I
believed that all of our ways are material for poetry, both in green
fields and in junkyards.

   I have waited in loneliness while a poem struggled to say what
cannot quite be said. I have tried to save for my books the poems that
spoke most clearly with my voice.

Snake in the Strawberries

UNPUBLISHED

Land of Beginnings

The door you once closed lets you slip through
back on the way from where you have come
to feel the soft earth of the land you plowed,
(kneel, old believer) between finger and thumb.

Here corner posts marked the farm's boundary lines.
I push one and feel it move, loose with decay
like a worn rotten tooth, the fence wires stripped off,
to merge field into field, the fashion today.

Scarcely a foot of this ground hasn't been
under your foot and your team and machines,
where you ended the days of labor and sweat
and learned the hard lessons a harvest means.

You find your hand shakes as it pulls up a weed,
in your land of beginnings. When all's done and said
if it still seems like home you may as well stay,
so plow yourself a furrow and plow yourself a bed.

Instead of Honey

Let's get to work, time may be short with us,
clouds hang trembling from a lip of sky,
the wind waits behind the distant wood.
We lean on the arms of summer, and as bees
ruffle the clover blooms we search for a storm
of flavor to melt on eager tongues.

Dig for yourselves, turn the earth,
miraculous manna waits on your need
for last judgments when meadows lie down
in a tempest of frost, when the sun
runs south on wounded feet, when sap
dries in green veins. Who'll shovel your way
into heaven? Not I, my labor's too dear.

Come, spit on your hands,
those muscles tied to your head,
teach them. I tell you the day
crouches beside us watching,
and you are not saved.
Let the spade welcome the hand
that builds on rock.

Something Not Tamed in Us

Early this winter morning
I saw two cock pheasants stroll
out of our patch of woods to feed
on corn my wife had scattered under
pine trees for the squirrels.
They moved with leisurely step
and pecked at the corn in such
a regal manner you would think
it was a favor to us for them
to eat our corn.
The little birds, the juncos,
chickadees, nuthatches, sparrows,

4

even cardinals and bluejays crowded
the porch feeder, squirrels rummaged
in the snow for buried nuts,
a rabbit stretched up to gnaw
the bark on a young apple tree.
But these are old acquaintances,
pensioners we've cared for for years;
they know where their welfare lies.
But the pheasants, newcomers,
majestic in bronze and purple vestments
made us feel alive in ways hidden
beneath daily banalities as if we
tapped some spring in a wilderness
hidden in our lives and out gushed
the waters of our beginnings.

Retirement Time Is the Time to Retire

About twilight, swallows stitched
the air, whine of insects almost too
high pitched to hear, cornfields breathed
moisture into an Iowa sky where
thunderheads caught the last rays
of sunset. He balanced on the hind legs
of an old chair he kept by the garden
for thinking and resting. Tonight the
slaughter of weeds around the tomatoes
gave him more sweat than comfort.
He lay back to squint at the first star
and tell himself to shape up, other men
had plowed their last furrow, left the field
and closed the gate. But he felt pushed aside,
worn out, not needed by love and labor.
Once he had joked about this day when
it lay far ahead in some misty future.
Suddenly it faced him, here, now.
He bent over to tie his shoe and the words
of an old farmer came to his mind:
The time to plant corn is at
cornplanting time.

5

To Build a Fence

We stretch a barbed wire from corner post
to corner post, 160 rods, half a mile.
It's a line to go by, even so we step back
a few rods and sight over the tops of the
posts already set to line up the new post.
Who wants a crooked fence and wouldn't
the neighbors chuckle. We turn the auger and dig
a hole two and a half feet deep and hope
for no rocks or tree roots to block the
twisting blade (tree roots are the devil,
you need an ax for them). We sweat and
place a post in the hole (creosoted post
that won't rot—we hope), line it up and
tamp the dirt in as if we planted it.
The corner post takes the most care,
it has to stand the strain of the tight
stretched wire all the way. We set it in
concrete, brace it against another post,
tie them together with strands of wire
twisted so tight it sings. One post has my
initials and date scratched in the cement.
We hung a gate on that one too. We staple
to the posts a thirty six inch woven wire
with three barbed wires on top. That's what
holds the outside out and the inside in.
Simple, as if the farm insists on order.

Grandfather and the Evangelist

A tent with a platform and with folding chairs,
a different church than the one where we belonged,
Grandfather held my hand, said I would hear
a deep-voiced man climb up the golden stairs.

Grandfather said I ought to hear a preacher
who sanctified himself with anecdotes
of Me and God and sold religion to all
like a medicine man, not like a prophet and teacher.

6

Grandfather said it was time I saw how sinners
can be relieved of guilt and dollars too.
"Woe unto you" was the fare Grandfather said
the saved sheep ate before their Sunday dinners.

I blushed and trembled when the big voice thundered,
"The devil lifts the skirt and fills the glass
show him no mercy and reap your reward in Heaven."
(And would they lift skirts there and drink, I wondered.)

He had me all mixed up. I couldn't find
the reason to be saintly here on earth
and take your pleasure when you got to Heaven;
it seemed to me he had this on his mind.

Grandfather said as he took me by the hand,
"Experience is the way you understand."

Not to Be Overlooked

We had a bull calf born premature,
never amounted to much, we kept him
in a small pen, remembered to feed him
and bed him down. Sort of a runt, he came
to be a fixture like forks and baskets.
Oh, we rubbed his head when we went by,
and checked on feed and water. But one day
when he was about six months old,
he backed off in his pen, took a run for it,
smashed the gate, hightailed it
through the barn knocking forks from
the racks, upset a basket of oats,
found an open door and ran wild around
the barnyard. It took four of us
to corral him and herd him back to his pen.
There he lay, quiet and serene as if
nothing had happened.
And I thought, I know folk like that
who have to show off just to prove,
I guess, that they are here.

Arrogance of Things

The growth of the cornfield today
answers yesterday's question,
but tomorrow? No guarantees beyond
the moment. A dark cloud with a
blast of hail tells me destruction
waits for no man. A touch of frost
will wither oak trees, cornfields,
living flesh. It is the stones,
bricks, machines that go on and on
in the arrogance of existence.
Even this typewriter and desk will prove
more durable than my nerves and muscle.
Dishes, for god's sake, outlive the hand
that cleans them. No wonder kings filled
their graves with possessions. Who wants
things (bought, stolen or given), to squat
like idols before the future's greedy eyes?
It may be the junkyard will get us all,
people, crops, tools, machines, but now
my fountain pen which I could snap in two,
mocks me with no signs of age. Swear or weep,
the shadow of the sundial haunts the human face.

Barns in November

Along an empty road I watched the barns
Crouched on the hillsides while the morning light
Poured in among the trees like mist and fitted
Panes to the windows now locked winter tight.

And overhead a birdless waste went streaming
Missed the sharp trees and mirrored with its own
Our rolling hills, but not in that grey country
Rise roofs like these, low bent and rooted in stone.

The bare and tattered fields have long been empty
Empty the pasture too of all save weather
Sowing his measure of snow where side by side
Fences and stones and furrows sleep together.

After the death of summer the barns inherit
Blossom and leaf and stem; granary and mow
Shoulder their loads in the darkness of timbers speaking
And pigeons sobbing. Winter is coming now.

And so the rafters arch to loosen the bony
Long fingers of the wind pressed toward the warm
And yellow pens where little calves lie sleeping
Rescued from their first snow. The heart of the farm

Beats in a slow beat and is steady, the pulse awakens
Strength in the beams and sills, and the haymow floors
Stretch their feet to the walls and a staring window
Discovers the farmer hastily starting his chores.

Thus shall the heart against a bitter season
Guard countless doors and windows, bring to bin
The crops of its own raising and gather in
The fruit and seed of love, the stalks of reason,

And stand alone among the vacant meadows
Calmly awaiting the age of winter weather
When, through the air, a chill and cloudy Heaven
Drops from its mantle of snow the first fine feather.

But the Earth Abides

The windmill squeaks, flaps broken vanes,
The barn needs paint, gates sag, weeds grow,
A manure pile leans against a shed,
Everywhere seeds that decay's hands sow.

But good news, good news, a new owner comes
With his bride, paint cans, new fangled machines,
Where the old man gave up the ghost and left
Once more clover learns what the sickle means.

9

A Secret to Live By

In the attic of my mind
sits a trunk packed with the
clothes of old ideas, also
age-yellowed snapshots of friends,
relatives, sweethearts taken in
fair and cloudy weather. The baggage
memory keeps, a broken birdcage
of a canary whose neck I wrung
in some childish rage, the usual litter,
dust, mouse droppings, a dead bat,
a basket of broken toys. But hid
under the eaves, hidden away,
lies a sealed envelope that holds
a secret I wrote to bolster my faith
in the traffic and market we live in.
Once I had a revelation of an
instinct for order in things great and small
that rang a bell for meaning I still try
to hear above the jostle of the street.

Routine

The boy drowning under waves
of sleep felt his father's voice
pull him to the surface again
and again until he crawled up
the beach toward morning chores.
He fumbled with both feet in one
overall leg, shirt tail dragging.
The morning sang with sunshine,
with birds, with pigs squealing,
with a neighbor's dog, clear but
distant. Winking mirrors of dew
scattered the light, vanes on the
windmill wheel blazed as it turned.
The cows to milk, cows, cows, where
were the cows? He rode the long-legged
pony with her halter, too bleary-eyed
to find the bridle. The cowpath

threaded its way through the pasture,
he galloped, a few cows ambled toward
the barn, others stood or lay apart.
Sullen with sleep he cursed them, his
shrill words whipping the air. It rose up
in him, the indignity of forced waking,
his anger hurt him with father's voice.
Sullen with sleep he beat
the pony over the ears and she
promptly threw him. He walked
behind the cows in his bare feet,
warm cowflops squishing between his toes.

Need For Magic

After a lonely night and an empty day
while neighbors talk of politics and weather,
you finally admit she's left you and you seek
a spell that will bring a man and his wife together.

You try to make up a recipe for magic,
of remembered things, her hands like folded wings,
hair curling from under her scarf on rainy days,
her awkward pose while she reads what the mailman brings.

And her words, her words, oh, any common phrase,
letters she wrote you starting with Dear Love,
notes to herself she often scribbled down
on a calendar that hangs beside the stove.

It might add enchantment to touch what she has touched,
straighten a picture, empty a vase, the door
to her closet to shut, her gloves on the davenport
tucked in the cushions, attempt a household chore

the way she did, for ingredients of the charm,
clean out the fireplace, polish the kitchen chrome,
wash a few windows and act as if you are sure
this spell shaped like a prayer will bring her home.

No Symbols

The barn's warm breath
smelled of pigs, straw, dust,
fresh manure. The night wind
rattled doors, poked fingers
under sills. The sow heaved and
grunted. He waited for an end
to waiting, the sow stretched
at his feet, her swollen belly
heaving. He reached into her
with two clumsy fingers, felt
tiny sharp toes not yet in this
world, tried to grasp them but
they slipped back. He shrugged off
his gunny sack shawl, ready to help.
He burned a match along a wire
with a loop and sharp hook.
Gently, tenderly, slowly he
inserted the hook and locked it
into the jaw of the unborn pig.
His finger in the loop he pulled
in time with the sow's labor,
brought the first pig through the
door to the outside. He watched
six more come kicking out
of their shells. A ray of light
shaped the window, shadows are born old.
The pigs rooted the sow's nipples,
if there was more meaning than that
he was too tired to care.

1937

Fall Plowing

The claim the stubble had no longer defends
This field, and mice laid bare in shallow burrows
Dart through the listless grass; a plow extends
Its shoulders of steel and the field goes back to furrows.

Slowly weeds stiffen to ash. All day the breeze
Cools the blazing sumach and rustles light
Syllables of death from frigidly burning trees
In each dry leaf that falls, in every blackbird's flight.

Autumn, Autumn, I can feel your harsh beauty
Closing around me as the end of the year
Moves into place to the sound of falling leaves,
I too have deaths to honor and the passion of death;
While grief sings in a shaking bush, while fear
Hunts in the furrow, my monuments arise
Like sudden shadows under October skies.

Poems appear by date of publication, not by date of authorship.

13

The Reason for Stars

I never wonder a lot about stars.
I'm much too busy with things of this earth
That show when a season of labor is done
Just what the labor's been worth.

Stars are all right to admire like flowers,
I like to see pretty things when I'm done
Working in fields, but what do I care
Whether a star is a stone?

There's plenty to learn in the ways of a seed.
What do you get if you study the sky?
I'm greater for holding one fruit in my hand
Than a heaven of stars in my eye.

Mad Dog

Like a great yellow dog, the sun
laps up the water in the creeks,
and his hot panting breath curls the corn
and sears the pasture brown.

He runs wild through the dry summer
as if no master could whistle him back,
or drive him to cover
in a kennel of clouds.

Cows Bawl on Sunday

The image of God
in a warm mackinaw and rubber boots
daily fights his way into the streaming barnyard
into a multitude of hungry, angry, playful
    and determined animals
through a cloud of raging sound
to bring order out of chaos.
Six times a week and rests not on the seventh—
and there fails his divinity.

Winter Field

Whether or not the man who turned
These furrows and wondered if in spring
He would be here with his team and seed
Still lives, after all, is the major thing.

For a field can always grow up to weeds
If it isn't plowed and levelled for grain,
But a man who's dead has no such luck
He's done with things like growth and gain.

So I, the man who plowed the field,
Shall be relieved when they are gone,
This winter sleep, this snowy death,
I'm ready for work when the spring comes on.

Clover Swaths

My eyes are cloudy with death.

I saw thirty acres of clover fall over the sickle bar
today (not the Grim Reaper, but a bright steel sickle
out of IHC, guaranteed for sixty days against
faulty or defective workmanship).

Thirty acres of clover in full bloom died today,
besides such incidentals as a hen pheasant with
both legs cut off, her eggs decorating horses' hooves,
and only God can count the number of bobolinks
and meadowlarks that find their world levelled.

Thirty acres of clover just in its prime,
in its greatest flower, this field—
lusty, sweet smelling, the seed nodes filling. . . .

Tonight when I go for the cows
I shall see it lying there in flat definite swaths.

(Only the young men go to war.)

15

In April

This I saw on an April day:
Warm rain spilt from a sun-lined cloud,
A sky-flung wave of gold at evening,
And a cock pheasant treading a dusty path
Shy and proud.

And this I found in an April field:
A new white calf in the sun at noon,
A flash of blue in a cool moss bank,
And tips of tulips promising flowers
To a blue-winged loon.

And this I tried to understand
As I scrubbed the rust from my brightening plow:
The movement of seed in furrowed earth,
And a blackbird whistling sweet and clear
From a green-sprayed bough.

Protest

Now as imperceptibly
As evening closing into night,
    As a young heart growing old
Is the wheatfield's sturdy green
    Shading into harvest gold.

The beauty of the color is
Not the thing which I protest,
    Gold is good when green is done—
But the summer in the sheaves
    Marks a season gone.

1943

Snake in the Strawberries

This lovely girl dressed in lambswool thoughts
dances a tune in the sunshine, a tune like a bright path
leading to that soft cloud curled up like a girl
in her sleep, but she stops at the strawberry bed
carrying nothing but joy in her basket and it falls
to the ground. Oh-h-h-h-h, her red lips round out
berries of sound but the berries under her feet are
not startled though they sway ever so slightly
as life long-striped and winding congeals into
form, driving its red tongue into her breast
forever marking its presence and turning into a shiver
barely a thread of motion in the clusters of green leaves.
She stands now as cold as marble now with the thought
coiled around her, the image of her thought holding her
tightly in its folds for it is part of her now and dimly
like faint sobbing she knows that part of her crawls
forever among green leaves and light grasses, it is the same
shiver that shakes her now and now her hair tumbles slightly
and now she feels dishevelled but the spell breaks finally.
For the warm sun has not changed and maybe the tune
of her coming still floats in the air but the path
no longer ends in the cloud. She fills her basket taking
the richest ripe berries for this is what she came to do,
she touches her breast a minute and then the ground
feeling beneath her fingers the coiled muscles
of a cold fear that seems so dark and secret
beside the warm colors of the sunlight
splashing like blood on the heaped fruit in her basket.

17

The Vine

His wife and young son in his heart, the future riding his
    shoulders
he eagerly plowed up the weeds at the rate of four miles an
    hour,
shuttling across the field on his shiny bright red tractor.
The cornfield around him proudly shone in the sunlight
as he turned to look at it proudly reflecting his gaze
while the wind like a wave washed the field into motion.
A young farmer riding an engine could plow up the world
especially in June, in the morning, the sunshine thick in
    his pulses.
But he stopped at midmorning to stretch his legs and
    discover
a coiled vine snakelike climbing and choking a cornstalk,
he picked at it, tore it away, looped it tight in his knuckles
and saw that it made a green handle holding him to the
    earth.
He studied it for a moment as if he'd abruptly abandoned
his iron rooster to fight back the wilds with his hands.
He tested the torque of the vine, and the suck of the roots
tightening the strings in his forearm. As if they were equals
they faced each other, a man and a wild morning glory
each with his claim on the earth.

When the vine could hold on no longer it snapped off
    clean at the ground
the white root writhing as the taut green curls
slowly untwisted slackening their pull on his fingers
and he shook them off with the thought, it will grow back
    again,
the root got away from me and its life is still there.
He turned to the power tied to the ends of his levers
to his own ways and emotions as live and green as the
    cornfield's
thrusting into the air in bannered flowers of existence
while under his feet coiled a strength he had not overcome.

Homesickness

Marie Summers took a course in Commercial
and a diploma landed her in the city candling eggs
where the elevated's roar was like music
and pavements moved under her feet on rollers
until spring came without spring's features
and turned loose the lonesome hounds.
At last she dried her eyes and went home
and the boys clotting the drug store
sniffed her sophistication eagerly.
But Marie only wept like a fool
at the sight of Monday's washing on the line
cookies cooling on the table
and a sun that walked like a giant
on everybody's grass.

After the Son Died

The trees follow two sides of a square
and make a fine windbreak
in this snug corner
apple trees mount the earth and sift their petals
over the stone foundation
over a pile of measured stone
where no house stands
these are just the roots of a house
but there is no growth
here is a background for living
and no life but these trees
and the rabbits who spout from the stones
like furry ghosts
no dream even stands here on this foundation
for the dream went under another stone
and a rented house in town is good enough now.

The Fence Row

A ripple of ground still shows the line where
a fence once divided this field in two—
the habit of being divided fades slowly
and may not be smoothed out in one growing season.

Here where two fields shared a common boundary
that kept corn from oats and the meadow from rye
the limit set to please some farmer's business
has now been plowed over and planted to crops.

There were stones here once and woodchuck burrows,
these things belong to the edge of a field,
where perhaps wild grapevine had looped protection
around the nest where the hen pheasant sat,

and rested its vines on the barbed wire fence
that stood for authority once in this place
till the wire went slack and the barbs grew rusty
and posts rotted off, and soon nothing was left

in the wave of the ground but a few wild roses,
though lately I found a freshly dug den
where a fox of the old school loyal to his party
had refused to admit that the fence row was gone.

The Neighborhood

The neighborhood has a mind and heart of its own
that do not meet the stranger frankly.
Meanings run hidden like underground streams
which well up in pools and angry fountains
when a housewife takes a lover
or a man is smothered in debt
or becomes blasphemous
or when a young boy or girl is touched
by the finger of death.

Time Like a Hand

The hardware merchant reaches back for the past
through the young girl's body
on a lonely road known as lovers' lane,

while the relentless hand of time at his back
pushes him down the street of middle age
where the picnic fires go out
and the green banks fade.
Where he is trapped behind the counter
with his washing machines
and annual conventions,

to watch the fat jovial days
vanish in the mirror of a grey skinned man
dressed in old promises.

Stranger

Following his father's footsteps
Clem Murphy retired at fifty
and left his boy on the farm—
but he is unhappy,
a stranger in a strange land.
The little Iowa town stares curiously
at Clem's ideas, its Chamber of Commerce
invokes the soot of factory chimneys
hoping to grow up into a second Chicago
out of the egg cases of the farmers.

Boundary Lines

The dog has a squirrel up a tree.
I can call off the dog, he will obey me
but the squirrel will not let me relieve him of fright
he clings to his branch until I'm out of sight,
willing to let our separate worlds whirl
where one creature is man and another is squirrel.

1951

Invocation

Come, you farmers, let us sing together
let us sing of the passion for planting
we the sowers and growers
live for the rising shoot and the spread root.

Let us sing a song of penance
for the ageless passion for crosses
staining the thick page of history
where we the peace lovers
fed and clothed the armies
where we the home lovers
milled like cows at the crossroads.
Let us sing low and sadly now
for the bellies not fed, the bare bed,
for rotten cotton and mouldy wheat
piled unfit to eat.

Let a Judas tree stand in every farm yard
to drop its bloody bloom at Easter time
come, you farmers, Easter is also
the marriage of sun with the earth,
but a Judas tree in every garden
all you land lovers who lie down at night
on a bed spiked with mortgages,
you crazy farmers who trade a whole generation
for a piece of ground,
come, let us sing together under our Judas trees,
we of the strong backs and deep voices
let us sing about our farms.

The Oracle

The oracle whose customer I am
Hides in the bottom drawer among my shirts
Or back of curtains, or upon the desk
Behind my unpaid bills, my solemn debts.

She won't take questions that aren't ready-made.
And neatly wrapped, delivered to my door,
She sends two answers, both ambiguous,
And I can choose the one on which I swear.

But still the morning seems like afternoon,
And floors I walk on echo underneath,
My oracle has told me I should take
Things just the way they are and save my breath.

Memorial Day

It puzzles me to see the stooping people
Bottling emotions in a vase of flowers,
The hurrying housewife and the stolid farmer,
The banker and the clerk, these friends of ours

All paying a respectful annual visit
To relatives tucked snugly underground
Who have no choice but entertain the callers
And hold the wilting blossoms on their mound.

There is no sign of welcome or refusal,
We set against each stone its sweet bouquet,
And satisfied at last with the arrangements
Solemnly start our cars and drive away.

Accident

The iron teeth of the harrow
gnaw the soft clods,
level the ridges,
and smooth the field,
rake through a killdeer's nest
without stopping,
and swallow the young birds.
The earth flows darkly past,
the tractor bone-jars on,
the heat waves wavering sing,
the killdeer build their nest again
low in the ground.

Farmer to His Son

Choose your wife for straight legs and honest tongue.
Take to market no more than you have to sell.
Be cautious with strangers and cover the top of your well,
And teach your children virtue while they are young.
And when you are old be glad if you've learned to keep
Your wife's affection and memories of neighbors and friends
And had the sense to know that your comfort depends
On the money you saved and the grief you have put to sleep.

Statement

It doesn't matter what the critics say,
I write what interests me in my own way.
I know they have to fill up the reviews
With what is called the literary news
But you and I have our own thoughts to please
And as my poems go by I hope you seize
On one or two that make you nod your head
As if you liked them. Poet Yeats once said
Of poetry and the critics' wailing wall,
"It's not a matter of literature at all."

24

Threat of Weather

We know we can outlast the weather
the two of us, it has stormed before.
We have been through worse times together
and not turned back, ice seals the door

while the wind throws angry floods of snow
in malediction against our walls
and tries to blind a clear window
through which, we hope, the warm light falls,

such as it is, for you to see
if you are out in the dark. We give
what comfort there is in knowing we
are willing to show you where we live.

As if to defy the wind I poke
the burning logs, the rising cry
of a startled fire through the chimney's throat
drowns out for a moment the wind's reply.

Let the house shake, our fire and light
still prove to us, as the books contend,
that two in love can accept the night
and not be afraid how it will end.

I learned resistance from a heart
of oak that lay charred in the grate,
it was in the fire from the very start
and still is solid. It's getting late

but here I'll say at the risk of turning
a first-rate farmer into a dunce,
it kept back enough for another burning
it didn't let everything go at once.

After Chores

Close down, Night.
Henry Jensen has finished his chores
and his lantern goes bobblesway bobblesway
flick-flick-flickering through long determined legs
saying, what has been said and done today has been
    done and said forever.
The worn familiar doorknob reaches out to his hand
and the house draws him in.

Now is the time to relax under the lamp, to fall asleep
over the evening paper. Unroll muscles, and stretch.
Too soon you will stiffen into the last position.
What is this? porkpotatogravybread and butter
    standing ahead
of applesauce and three fat raisin cookies?
Reach out your hands, Henry Jensen, unleash your
    hunger . . .
tell me, is anyone tireder than a tired man
eating his supper?

O sleep drugged head, staring endlessly
past murderers marriages crop reports and the
    stubborn fact of local items
hold up, hold up, the world confesses itself before
    your eyes
and you sink lower in deep clutched hands seeking
    the pillow.

These are the hours that no one counts when time
sneaks past your chair like a cat and the reluctant foot
has not yet found the stair
has not yet made
one quiet footstep further toward the night.

1962

Love

Love hungers, a cruel eye
stalking from the cliffs of cloud
the trembling sign—a meadow heart
is pinned beneath its plunging shadow;
goes with a rush of wings
into thick cedars at dusk
fiercely and no cry is lent
the wind where talons
struck.

The Unprotected

The sun at noon
stirs a scurry of ants
to autumn's business.
I wear my owner's look today
and charge the bins and granaries
with the field's account. I'm trustee of
a township in my heart where summer joy
and spring expectancy depend on schools
of singers, cheepers, chirpers, clowns in grass
and pool and air, who chorus, caper alive
the spirit's moments. And now I must provide
against the day when snow lies deep,
the sun shrinks south, and no kind neighbor comes
breaking the drifts to say the year has turned.

27

Truth

How the devil do I know
if there are rocks in your field,
plow it and find out.
If the plow strikes something
harder than earth, the point
shatters at a sudden blow
and the tractor jerks sidewise
and dumps you off the seat—
because the spring hitch
isn't set to trip quickly enough
and it never is—probably
you hit a rock. That means
the glacier emptied his pocket
in your field as well as mine,
but the connection with a thing
is the only truth that I know of,
so plow it.

Many Hens Do Not Make Light Work

The drake has too many hens
and he knows it.
They squat meekly
supplicating favors
with sleepy eyes
and soft necks.
He bows loyally many times
and shakes his tail
up and down like a
salt sifter to put himself
in the mood. But, alas,
he treads the warm
willing backs with
every hope of achievement
but his promise wavers
and he falls back,
waddling off like a man
late for a committee meeting.

The Shadow

I have seen the butcher's shadow
Point like a finger where I live
Unguarded in my house of peace,
And I wept in fear.

I would rather sleep in desert places
Grow thin, unwanted, scorned, denied,
Bearded, strange, too dry for friendship,
Brother of bees and locusts,

Than be a sacrifice upon the altar
Built by the lust for self-destruction,
Where the smoke corrupts our breath
And prayers drip fat as the fire ascends.

Let me stand free, not chained by hate,
No bullock crowned with thorny flowers
Brushed and sleeked by adoring eyes,
Led by the doomsday priests to a darkened room
Where the shaggy air rank with death
Hooks at my heart with an old dilemma.

Moment toward Spring

This is the day when on the hills of noon
The winter's towers burn, the torchman sun
Makes virtue of destruction as he strikes
Flame to the drifts and melts them one by one.

And everywhere the tyranny is broken,
The shining fields appear, the poplars stand
Ready to publish leaves, the messenger pigeons
Rise from the barn and circle over the land.

I stare from my door amazed at the resurrection
Of rising life where the snowbank burned, I note
A fire more fierce and strange than ever I set
Under a kettle to pulse in the chimney's throat.

The Old Admonitions

The friend that I had
Marched away to the war
And the girl that I loved
Turned me out of her door,
And the taste of my life
Without friend, without wife,
Went sour at the core.
The minister muttered,
"Man reaps what he sowed."
But the old admonitions
Are dust in the road,
Are as useless to me
As the wind in the tree,
As the big-bellied, arrogant
Wind in the tree.

Birthplace

This is the heart of the farm where I was born,
This farmhouse framed in remembered feelings of home,
Here is the window where first the sun spied me,
Here are the elm trees that told me about the wind.

I stand in the yard where once in imitation
Of my father's six-horse team on the big gang plow
I hitched our collie dog to my baby cart
Which he overturned and licked my face when I cried.

I think how many autumns the leaves have fallen,
How my folk have fallen, and friends and neighbors too
Have loosened their hold on time and drifted away
Leaving the work of their hands for me to remember.

Here is the hoe my grandfather often used
Until it wore down thin as an iron shaving,
Here is the rug grandmother wove and kept
When she went upstairs to die on her walnut bed.

And the rose an aunt had painted, the raffia wreaths
Hung on the walls to be used as picture frames,
The copy of "Snowbound" faded and gently worn
That belonged with the apples and fire to a winter night.

I lay my hands on the Bible, heavy and black,
That spoke to me sternly on Sundays about my sins,
So that I had a solemn face as I did the chores
And wondered if I could be trusted another week.

The hitching post is gone and the stepping block.
The view from the window is changed, the trees have grown,
They bury in shade the porch where mother planted
A rambler rose to surround each ornate post.

The lawn seems shrunken where once my cousins played
At forbidden games as well as hide-and-seek,
And how they admired my father who let them ride
An old plow horse that was very suspicious of children.

The horse has melted to earth but the mouldy saddle
Still hangs in the barn, I tremble to think how things
Outlive the hands that used them, they speak to me
In the voice of a teacher echoing down the years.

The fields remember the past where children knee deep
In shooting stars saw ditches drain the sloughs
Now fenced and fertile but rimmed by the same horizons,
A land known by the signature of the plow.

If the roots of the present seem reaching down to the past,
The upthrusting plants insert their tips in my heart,
For this is the earth where I grew in sunshine and storm
And learned from rocks to bear time's levelling blows.

My sister and brothers and I mocked the farm's slow pulse
Locked deep in our veins when the sun awarded us shadows,
But it keeps its account in stray sheaves pledged to the gleaner
From a stubble field green-leaved in our early season.

Limited View

The clutter and ruck of the stubble publish the time
That prompts my steps, I know what I have to do
For my bread before frost locks the land against
My hand, and fire shoulders the chimney flue.

Rocks have a word that crows repeat over and over
On the cold slopes of winter where the picking is poor,
It echoes in empty granaries and I learn by heart
To say in the hard days to come, endure, endure.

But now I straddle the field and break its back
In the vise of my plow, while a thresh of weather streams by
Sweeping up clouds and birds, leaves, banners of smoke;
I gouge out furrows, a starved wind ransacks the sky.

Change toward Certainty

The afternoon closed in until it seemed
No larger than a room of snow and cloud,
The small March sun glowed dimly in its socket,
The window of the air looked out on mist.
I met you there among the apple trees
Close to the feedlot where the playful steers
Rumpled the bedding in their narrow pen,
And starlings searched the ground for spilled out grain
Like careful business men, the fog was a wall.
Oh, we were all prisoners of the day
Though some found fences more substantial than
The feeling. I was centered in my mood,
Your warm appraising look slid off my back.
Like quicksand underneath our boots the snow
Shifted as we sank deeper in our coats.
Look, and you pointed to a maple tree
Where swollen buds now showed a waxy red,
I looked from where bare ground defied the frayed
Snow carpet, then you said, There's not much yet.
I felt the wind, not freezing, raw and wet.

32

A ghostly crow in the fog spoke his short piece
With nothing new to say, I looked at you
And saw your hair curl lively from your scarf
Framing your face where the excitement grew
Out of an anxious frown as if a light
Had come to light blind eyes, your mittened hand
Turned snug in mine like a child's while a shadow went
Away from your face, and the actual bodies of things
Filled up the space where their shadows had seemed to be.
Nothing seemed changed and yet the change was there
In the tree, in the bird, in you and I felt your love
Beat in me like a pulse I had always known.

The Visit

(FOR ROBERT FROST)

The little world of the garden bare,
Swept by the frost from wall to wall,
We carry our roots to the cellar's bin
When, look! a brown thrush comes to call.

The short day runs on frozen feet,
Its shadows lengthen out ahead,
But today a gentleman in brown
Sings in our hedge, pecks at our bread.

All through the night we hear the surge
And ebb of wind against the panes,
Housed in his twigs and straw our guest
Startles us with his summer strains.

The morning climbs its shrunken arch,
The sun dial wakes, but the bird is gone
As if he had told us all he dared
Of life renewed by the grace of song.

Late Meadowlark

We know the meaning when we read the signs
in sumac leaves but still abides the wish
to halt leaf fall, to sweep the frost from grass,
and beckon back the winging flocks
that waver from sight.

But look, look here, here in the yard,
alone, unafraid, in a stack of straw,
a meadowlark crouches and tries its tune
as if one voice whose truth is summer
could strike its pitch and sing back days
born of the sun. I smile, of course,
for birdlike faith, but even I,
calendar read and learned in texts,
hearing this song find my taste hungers
on autumn's table for a peach out of season.

Scatter the Petals

She sleeps as if the mouths of buds
About to utter their gentle bloom
Suspended breath lest an echo darken
The silence where she keeps her room,

And sleeps. The warm October sunlight
Holds in its hands the troubled year's
Moments of grace before they wither
The asters, and leaves rain down like tears.

She seems to dream in the early shadow
Where a fountain trembles, she does not start
At the blackbird's whistle above the cedars
Nor the tiptoe steps of my anxious heart.

I bow my head as the prayers attend her,
But heart, poor innocent, swells to make
A sudden gesture of warning to tell me
At the last farewell, she will not wake.

34

1967

Men Give More than Promises

You'd let me walk barefoot on
broken glass while you wore shoes,
you'd wring the necks of baby birds,
if the mother bird was watching,
to show how strong your muscle is,
I might have died and if I had
you'd have bought paper flowers and
thought you showed off big, you in a
new suit and straight face just long
enough to get me stuck away. Boy, when
you said, "You got yourself in this, now
work it out," I knew how much you cared.
I'd like to get you in a trap that
closed a little tighter every day
and watch you gnaw the bars, I'd take
you to that phony doc who cuts your
heart out while he springs you free,
and let you hobble down the street so
bugged with shame you hope the garbage
truck will pick you up—don't come near
me, snowing me with them words, you don't
love me, I'm just a doll, rag one at
that to play with. I'll nail my door
so tight death can't get in if you
come around again.

Love in Autumn

Do you remember the meadow
when clover bloom brushed your knees
and bumblebees arched their backs
to plunder flowers, your eyes
dreamy with sunlight as you tasted the honey
of late love? The air trembled with
your low song and the meadowlark
listened to catch the tune and the clouds
kept their shade from you, your hands with
the signs of work on them lay loose in your lap.
Autumn turned mellow with goldlight
and each day set a crown of sweet
purpose on your hair.
It was then I came from my work with the
stains of sweat still on me, ears alive to catch
my name, my hands eager for your touch,
and the hard lines smoothed from my face and
labor turned light and the stony ground
softened for the plow and even the plow handles
themselves seemed hung with tiny bells.

Forsythia

You said, take a few dry
sticks, cut the ends slantwise
to let in water, stick them
in the old silver cup on the
dresser in the spare room and
wait for the touch of Easter.
But a cold wave protected the
snow, and the sap's pulse beat
so low underground I felt no
answer in myself except silence.
You said, winter breaks out in
flowers for the faithful and
today when I opened the door
the dry sticks spoke in little
yellow stars and I thought
of you.

36

Elegy

Listen, Justesen, shuttered in
your small room, winter is gone.
I tell you spring now wakens
furred buds on the boughs of pussy
willows, at the field's edge a lark
nests among weed stalks harsh with
the wind's whistle. Maples unfold
new leaves, oaks wait for the warm
May sun, violets rise from the curled
clusters and wild plums cover thorns
with white blossoms, even watercress
shows color at the spring's mouth.
You have seen flocks of geese print
their flight on the wide innocent sky
over Iowa, and bundled farmers on bright
red tractors smooth the fields for sowing.
Listen, you can hear the cock pheasant's
cry while April rain sends up shooting
stars and jack-in-the-pulpits. Fill your
mind's eye with the hill beyond the big
barn where she last watched an autumn sunset.

Apple Harvest

The wind knocks on my door,
I must pick my apples now
or let them rot.
The wind straddles my back,
I set the ladder carefully
lest more than apples fall.
Someday the tree will die
and with stalks and men, towers,
birds and fruit seek earth's
level. We support our shapes
while our strength lasts. I store
the barrels inside the shed
and with my thoughts I watch
the clouds, gray membrane of wind
across the eye's vision.

Three Sides to a Farm

So now he wants to buy my farm, he's got
The girl—young squirt showing off how smart he is
He tries to be casual, off hand, man to man,
"An old bachelor like you," he says, "could move to town
"And take it easy, what do you want for your farm?"
I spurred him a little, just to see him jump.
"What do you want with a farm? You just got married.
"With a wife like that you won't have time to work."
He cocked his head, a grin on his big mouth
(I'd like to knock it back into his teeth),
"Marriage won't bother me none, she's a good girl
"But she's got to learn to work, money ain't free."
(Work? That child? Like putting a fawn in harness)
"One hundred and sixty acres will do to start with."
He boasted. Start with? My God, does that boob know
It took me forty years to get it paid for?
"I know you wouldn't cheat me, you've known me
"Since I was knee high to a grasshopper
"So I guess we can trust each other." Did
You ever hear such bleat? A milk-fed lamb
Sassing an old buck? "My wife has money,
"A little, I ought to be able to borrow the rest."
All right, you borrow and give me the mortgage, Boy.
I'll show you a trick or two, (that girl, that girl,
She shouldn't have let this young pup lick her hand).
"Me sell my farm? I might at that. Stiff price
. "On easy terms. Sure we've been neighbors, friends,
"Since you were born, a contract signed by you
"Would suit my book, with yearly payments made
"Of interest and principal." Then let him squirm
When he hits a year when he can't make the payments.
He'll treat her like a slave and let her sink
Into a dreary round of kids and chores.
(Oh God, if I had that girl I'd build a tower
Out of my love so deep and high and strong
She could only see the love and heart it's torn from.
I'd walk barefoot through glass to touch her hand.)
Listen and hear him stretch his yapping voice.
"It's all I need to start with, a quarter section,
"Make out the papers and show me where to sign."

Did you ever see such a fool? Like his father was
Who always trusted the man who cheated him.
Born as a sheep who wanted to lose his wool,
Well, I was glad to shear him and be obliging.
Let the boy sign, I'll hold him prisoner
To that signature like a vise, I'll let him see
(She had the softest hair when a little girl)
Once more how an old fraud leaves a line of tracks
In the snow of the new year.

Quarrel's Echo

The front steps seemed not
to remember my tread as if
she had told them to treat
me like a stranger. I pushed
the bell and felt the echo
of an empty house. I rang the
bell again but the locks obeyed
their orders and silence spoke
for the closed door. I turned
my back on the blank features
and told the steps good day,
and my wish not to be salt
kept me from the sight of her
pale face hiding in a window
while two sparrows bickered in
the eaves over a half-built
nest.

Tasters

The summer sun made blood like sap
rise till her lily face blushed red,
he felt the swell and wash of love
nuzzle his veins from toe to head.

In Eden's garden ripened fruit
dripped sweet between the lips, alas
birds sang a warning soft as breath,
the smart snakes gossiped in the grass.

Plea for Single Focus

You saw double today when you said you saw the wind
riffle the tree tops while the waters lay still—
there's always a child playing house or going up in a swing,
and an old man, lame or blind, going down hill.

Though the sun invades the summer burning with pollen,
the dark nights of winter lie heavy like flesh in pain,
there's always a picnic with a full moon on the river,
there's always hay to be made before the rain.

A farmer plants apple trees, his young son watches
from the stump of an old one cut down by an ax or time,
lilies bloom sweet in their beds before they fester,
bells describe weddings or funerals by their chime.

A man lifts walls of a new house set on a hillside,
sows grass to hide a raw grave with its feathery touch,
on a rickety porch in the valley a small helpless woman
rocks slowly, finds even that effort almost too much.

Oh, see with now's round-eyed appeal, hold and cherish
love's warm hands like wheat grains at harvest, sweet apples
        and red,
remember how water dissolves the dry desert's rancor,
that a vision turns stones of fact to miraculous bread.

Before Frost

Now summer's golden bell is mute,
the muffled tones of autumn sound,
this is the day we store the fruit
and search the ridges of the ground

for pockets of potatoes. Vines
of melon, squash, piled by the fence,
a zodiac of garden signs,
confirm the gardener's common sense

in recognizing portents, hot
odors of rotting cabbage stir
him as he watches mares tails blot
the sky and chestnut burst its burr.

Before frost speaks the final word,
he shapes the furrow to the plow
turning the earth whose harvest stored
in sack and basket waits him now,

as in the cellar of the heart
the roots of love lie safe and cherished,
the gardener sighs to end his part
with seeds and seasons that have perished.

Line between Seasons

The rollicking whinny of the wind
tunnels the arches of the trees,
itinerant snowdrifts hug the ground
and find diminished comfort there.

Buds are bundled tight as bulbs
as out of its pattern the grass unfolds
and deep roots pump the sap through veins
to open the leaves of a maple's virtue.

My neighbor, I know, has seen the signs
but he, by god, serves the commonplace,
go draw the line yourself, he says,
he keeps his pace but will not hurry.

Not being a willow, he only sees
(and knows what he sees, or says he does)
enough to follow his own concerns,
he won't change more than the change around him.

He studies the wintry clouds and waits
firmly convinced the sun's in season,
knee deep in the mud with a hold on March
he notes that a heifer has taken the bull.

Progress

Own all the land you can get,
tile the sloughs, blast the rocks,
burn the trees in the grove,
level the hills and bury the creek,
you bought it to make it pay, didn't you?
Fence it, fence it, heavy gauge woven wire
with three barbed wires on top—show
who's the owner. You can act like
a king and say, by god, what shall
be done and not done, what field plowed,
(even the old sod pasture) and which
one souped up with fertilizer. It's
your land, isn't it? Poison the gophers,
trap the raccoons, shoot the crows,
all enemies of profit, whose farm is it
anyway? You give it the works and get
used to the mortgage on your back.

And won't you be surprised some
morning, oh, who knows when, but later on
some fine morning a man like you with a
gimp in his leg, and a tricky heart and
shaky hands will pound in a stake and nail
a board on it that says FOR SALE.

Wilderness Ways

The rabbit knows the hawk is there,
the hawk sees where the rabbit hides,
the wilderness sustains the pair
with no pretense of choosing sides.

Nor does the deer choose hunter's ways
though hunter tracks a heart to death,
but hunted nor the hunter stays
the talon's plunge, the arrow's breath.

Undertow

The bay of morning shines through
night's thicket, no windpuffs ruffle
the surface, I swim a straight course
from breakfast table to desk and
survey the solitary beach where I work.
The storm dwindles in my mind to a
passing cloud, all about me lie the
signs of calm, the fresh odor of a
new day rises like a breeze through
pines, the instruments read steady,
direction north, temperature mild.
I settle myself for the day among
the cargo of my thoughts, stamping them
to ship out, when like a shell half
buried in the sand, I find the
handkerchief crumpled by your hands
behind my bookshelf. A sigh sends up
a wave so huge the undertow sucks me
from my mooring and floats me out to sea.

The Hunter

You cannot kill the white-tailed deer
With tears in autumn when the mellow wind
Fingers the apples and pulls down the grapes
One by one from the cluster, blows the frost
On breathy mornings into a comet's shape.

You cannot kill the white-tailed deer
With kindness no matter how your hounds
Worry them with affection, you will find
Trails through the empty woodlands like the bare
Patterns of their hoofprints in your mind.

You must be ruthless, hunter, and stalk them down
From behind the trees, in covert, blind and mire,
And slaughter them one by one as the hunter's moon
Bloodies its face with clouds of drifting fire.

43

Close the Accounts

The putting away time shows up
on the calendar after frost prompts me
to turn the page. I grease sickles,
back the mower into the shed beside
the plow and planter, coil the hayrope
on a hook inside the barn, turn off
the water at the pump that runs to
the pasture, drain the tanks there.
This is the day to straighten barn doors
with new hooks and hinges, fold back gates
to the fields and let the cattle glean
the empty rows, to file away spring's
expectations with heart's discontent.
Labor has dried its sweat and written
its sum under the year's account. I
read what the granaries say, walk
through my autumn thoughts under a shower
of yellow leaves, my gains less than I'd
hoped, my losses more than I planned.

The New Calf

In the basement by the furnace lies
a newborn calf I found, chilled and wet,
in the barn this morning, its mother
a wild-eyed young heifer frantic in
the pain of her first birth didn't
lick it off to dry its hair and kicked
it in the gutter when it tried to suck.
I picked it up, rubbed it down and
fed it from a bottle. Here it lies
in a basket lined with straw while
I watch its heart tremble, flanks quiver,
muzzle twitch, eyes flicker. It sucked
so feebly on my finger I had to spoon
the milk (mixed with a little brandy)
in its mouth and stroke its throat
to make it swallow. Now it waits for life

to decide whether to go or stay—and
I think of deserted innocence everywhere,
a child locked out of the house,
a woman dirtied in love,
a father betrayed by his son, all of us
sometime abandoned, lonely, denied.

Forewarned

Now when the breath of frost has chilled
The waiting aspens, when the sky
Has floated the birds to another country
And summer's brook goes dry,

I can review and list my losses
Without complaint, shoulder my grief
While the cold-fingered wind strips
My heart of its last leaf,

And watch time's plow turn under days
Like stubble, I must lace my boots
And fill the cellar bins—they winter,
Trees, in their roots.

Karma

Still, cries of hunting shake the grove
where as a boy I with my gun
betrayed a rabbit shy as love
who made no leap to hide or run.

Deep in the cleft where time returns
the man and weasel to one shape
and no star for those shadows burns,
the hands of love were claws of rape.

And I who walk convinced of grace
should flee in terror day and night,
prey to the hunter I must face
who will not loose me from his sight.

1968

Games Are Never Free

The city park still draws children
to its shabby ambush, leaves and
papers soak in the bird-stained
fountain, grass dies along swing
runways, trees scratch at clouds,
cries scalp Indian-hearted boys,
girls swing at the sky, small fry
clot the slide and scream their wonder.

    Lord, what a sight!
How many games ago I raced through
the forest until a father's voice
harried me home. Stern-faced houses
still surround the park, still frown
at my search through leaf-fall for
the path to my wilderness, remind me
games are never free, scold a
running boy who has forgiven me
many broken promises.

End of April

A grey sky roofs the morning
and just when I have decided
it is the only color the
day will wear, a tulip
bursts in my face, a boy
across the street hoists a
purple kite, a neighbor lady
arranges a clothesline with
plaid shirts and checked aprons,
an angleworm turns red on the
sidewalk, I flinch from the glance
of polished chrome.
If you were here, we would not
gawk at these flash cards but
follow the example of May baskets
and decorate our door with
surprise tendrils of love.

Here and There

It's true the days are longer
the sun didn't get caught under
December's dark horizon after all.
Buds in the maple seem swollen, signs
of an early spring lie out for all
to read, today breaks open with
sunlight, it makes no sense at all
to blunder in ravines or swear at
barred gates.
No fires burn in the streets, food
cascades from the market shelves,
water flows from faucets. . . .
The old man, homeless, naked, hand.
broken by torture, eyes sunk deep
in sockets, wanders in a season
where the sun contends with clouds
alive with bloody beaks and
extended claws.

1969

The Chipmunk and I

The chipmunk sits upright
(as some men do not)
and opens the peanut shell
at one end and with tiny hands
presses the nut into a cheek
swollen like mumps—the chipmunk
sequesters every nut he finds,
dim in all our veins rides the
spectre hunger. His stripes
(the chipmunk's) run up his back
to the end of his nose, his fur
is flecked with gold, his bushy tail
stands straight up, he jerks
like a wound-up toy. I watch him
sniff his way to the windfalls
I throw him and expect no thanks
or greetings. He eyes me as
nature's neighbor to be neighbored
at a formal distance. We know where
the line is drawn and keep
our own places.

Dogma

Sucked and bitten I shake
puppy questions from dry dugs
of thought, leave the kennel
classroom to the litter of students
and trot down the street alone.
Store windows shelter my reflection
as my eyes tiptoe around crowded faces,
I shrink at the call of a familiar voice,
gallop away from a proffered greeting,
pad on stealthy notions toward a cave,
lest I am caught without my collar
and no one calls my owner.

View by View

Poplars mark the limit of the yard,
in front the house is bounded by a street,
smoke rises from the chimney, snow falls down,
Saturday afternoons is when we meet.

One clock is silent but the other strikes,
even the stealth we practice has its rules,
your car's in plain sight but we lock the door,
wise men leave their tracks the same as fools.

Fast in the web spun by the spider love
you and I so entangled in what we do
and bound to each other wait on what's ahead
helpless before time's change from view by view.

1970

Resort to Calm

No protest, just the door's soft sigh,
but the house shocked me with its
closed blinds and stale breath.
I touched your hand, you smiled
and said, Let's go outside and sit
behind the hedge in sheltered privacy.
Your rolled your stockings down,
thrust out your legs, I shed my shirt,
we bathed in pools of sunshine.
The afternoon beamed on us, forsythia
lit its yellow fire, urgent odors
smelled of earth, spring's warm river
flowed through us, over us, around us,
and we talked as neighbors met by accident
who swap news in neighbors' fashion.

Routine Keeps Me

I make water in the morning
before I eat breakfast because
one need is greater than another,
but I don't shave unless I want to
until noon—routine keeps me

trimmed, neat, clean and fairly
comfortable, a credit to my profession,
a relief to my wife, a plus sign
to my banker and a recognition
by the neighbors that I will keep
my lawn mowed and dog tied.
But sometimes when I put on
my work clothes on Saturday and
my church clothes on Sunday, when I
see the dentist every six months,
the doctor once a year, and pay my
bills the first of each month,
buy Christmas presents before Christmas,
birthday presents a day late,
buy a suit in the middle price range,
a new car every third year, avoid
women at parties who seem too friendly,
and men who seem too cold, as I count
the expense of each risk and decide
it's too much, then sometimes I think
(not in working hours) of the mountain
ground-squirrel who hibernates eight
months of the year and wonder if
he ever wakes up out of season.

Discarded

I tried to open a drawer in
the old desk but something inside
braced against the frame, a book perhaps,
or a bundle of papers, or half-closed
ruler. I pushed and pried and jerked.
My thoughts said, Forget it! Nothing there!
But my clattering heart shouted,
Not so, Not so, there's an old letter
(pink fragile paper smelling of
rose petals) you used to read when
you were lonely. . . .
Today when the Good Will truck
came for the desk I remembered
the words "you" and "always" and "love."

1971

Sharers

You grieved so for a rosebush
frost killed, I brought you
a cinquefoil to grow in its place
and light with small yellow blooms
the gray space, we planted it in
fresh earth, tamped and watered it
with a gardener's pride, blessed it
with spring hope.
    Now in the autumn wind
we wrap the bush against the cold,
lest the sight we shared of small
yellow flowers desert us in
a barren spring.

A Misery Bleeds

A misery bleeds inside of me
today and will not let me be,
it is a day like any day,
subtract or add a small degree.

There must be something ails a man
to plague himself on this bright day
when what he wants is what he has
but what he has he will not say.

Out of Season

Half of the elms along the street look dead,
a smell in the air like garbage starting to rot,
crab grass muscled through lawns and army worms,
and no one mowed the weeds in the vacant lot.

Enough to make your stomach turn inside out,
everything running down and going to seed,
a world at war with itself, hell bent to die,
people so stingy I doubt if cut they'd bleed.

This nymph appears. I'm old, slack spirited.
She struts by short skirt almost to her crotch
and smiles at me and time breaks out in flowers—
in dreams I cut on my gun another notch.

Thought of Bluebells

Along the banks
back from the water's edge,
beds of bluebells lie ready
to transform the earth.
They sleep in their roots
until the spring sun
calls on them to bloom.
How many times you and I
have assumed their blue
assurance when our love
survived a cold season
with only its roots alive.

1972

Cock Pheasant

The pool of morning lay cool
and quiet behind the garden gate,
earth broke from its winter skin,
a white-faced moon retreated
down the sky, a shaggy oak kept
its dead leaves, if roots uncurled
from tulip bulbs and sap swelled
lilac buds they made no stir, even
the air warmed quietly in the sun.

Along Dry Run trees held bare twigs
without a sigh, arches of dead weeds
looped over the garden's edge, rotted stumps
of cabbage exhaled a sour breath, a row
of corn stalks crouched on stiff knees.

From a clump of thick grass
a cock pheasant shattered the
morning surface, exploded in purple
and gold as he rocketed through
sunlight, his hoarse yell broke open
the silence and suddenly color and
passion recovered the day for us all.

Alien

The winter trees replied
when the wind questioned them
but no words I understood nor
did they speak to me.
The barn humped its back
against the low sun and
threw a shadow across my path.
Melting snow trickled past
a manure pile, stained
the edge of drifts and a rat
busy in corn spilled from
the broken side of a crib
made the solitude bearable
as if to say the lesson learned
from hard facts should teach me
the consolation of hunger.

Cry Shame

Stones outlast weather,
horses sleep standing up,
flies never bother pigs—
how can I endure the tears
of a woman whose husband died
in a jungle?
I have my own wailing wall
to weep against for the many
murders I have planned, and
what sleep is there for any of us
when our hearts cry shame?
I too have sent planes, bombs, poison
to burn and rape the country
of brotherhood, and who can tell me
what to say when my own anger
calls me to account.

Destruction

The barn stood for shelter
on squared corners with a tight roof
until the wind sucked it up
and spit it out in a shambles
of splintered boards. I tried
to salvage the ruins. While I
pulled nails and sorted out
split studding, citizens of the
barnyard clustered around—pigeons
fluttered where once the ridge pole
hung, sparrows frisked through
broken window frames—and let me
sweat over the collapse of order.
I lit my pipe and tossed the match
toward the tumbled hay and let
chance decide if it lived or went out.
The flame caught, winked among the
stems, then tongued the air until
the draft formed a chimney and the
fire went mad. I leaned against a
corner post, the roar of the fire like music,
the lunge of its appetite now
beyond control.

The Farmer's Bride

Dry weeds wait for snow,
trees creak, the road's skin
turns gray, a pale sun throws
pale shadows, cold air wraps the day.
I see a bundled man in work clothes
walk across the yard, head bowed
to mark icy spots where a man
might fall, his mittened hands
hang like boards. The dog leaps

to lick his face, cats arch and
weave between his legs, the cows
moo softly at his approach, even
sparrows follow behind his back.
He does the chores before dark,
and locks the barn doors, warm in a
faith he shoulders with all he owns
that a spring sun will sometime
break the winter's back. I stand
and wait where a wound of light
bleeds through the window.

Sounds around a Man

It's late, late in the year
to hear a plowman sing, he yells
his tune above the tractor's clatter
mocked by a crow from its perch
in the grove. I listen to air shaped
to sound, a hunter shoots, a pheasant
squawks from the meadow and flashes
bronze and scarlet as he sails downwind,
a dog barks, somewhere a cow bawls,
two boys shout from a farm yard.
I grew up with this language hoping
to find what signs warn me what I
stand for, for whom I speak.
These bugle notes ring out in a
bowl of sky bound by horizon's
ring to solid earth, the plowman
rides over the hill with his song,
wind mutters among the dead weeds,
the power line overhead vibrates
its monotone, I am caught in a web
of voices anchored as far
as their echo.

1973

A Testament

That ant down there, dragging his leg,
pushes his crumb around stones,
cracks in earth, grass stems . . .
may not even see the sky.
No sign he asked for help,
his wife, the neighbors,
or complained that a good ant
now suffers, no Job of ants
on his dunghill to argue with God.
He seems to say,
you push your crumb and I'll push mine
with no questions asked.
I watch him drag that leg
around hills and down valleys
while he keeps the crumb moving
to push his luck home.

Revelation

Who ordained the flicker on my
metal ridgepole that he greets the
sunrise with such thunderous tattoo?
There he goes again, the hammer-voiced
prophet, rousing the neighborhood
to praise. Who wants to hear his
invocation at four o'clock in the
morning? The whole house shakes
with his fervor. Again and again
and again he calls us to witness.
Why can't he testify from a dead
branch for a mate and caterpillars?
And leave us to our own devotions
when we get our eyes open.

Day of the Cornfield

The day of the cornfield all right,
hanging ears kernelled by pollen
pulsing down hollow silks in the
slow ejaculation of creation.
In the book of earth the farmer
throws a giant shadow, his eyes
greedy, hands gnarled like roots.
Now he leans on the gate, strokes his dog,
tired with spent passion. He notes a
rabbit nibbling a fallen ear, a cock pheasant
slips between the rows, he quiets his dog,
his voice stuffed with yellow sounds of corn,
the heavy ears wrapped in their message
of the season.

1974

Auction

The house offers its private
life to the public eye with
fruit jars, china pitchers,
''Blue Boy'' in a gilt frame,
mouse traps, a brass bedstead,
dress model, hot water bottle,
button box, old leather couch, '
two sets of stereopticon views
of the Holy Land, a cradle,
steamer trunk, lace scarf—
strange hands claim them
who knows by what need, while
the auctioneer's hammer argues
the virtues of worn-out things.

1975

Portrait of an Old Horse

I wonder what shaggy thoughts
lie back of the long bony face,
trimmed forelock between half-cocked ears,
eyes bugged out bright as brown-skinned glass,
sagging lip—mine droops in the mirror
when I neigh the hungry hope
fleshed behind bony brows.
He stands there switching flies,
shoulders worn, sunken, collar sores
healed over with gray hairs
(my head full of gray hairs).
He pulled a plow, wagon, mower,
something, can't stop pulling,
he marches with a team as he
stands naked without his harness—
he'd go to meet a class even if
the classroom was empty,
what else could he do?
He never chased a butterfly
in his life or jumped a fence.
Now he's old, sway-backed,
scruffy-tailed, teeth smooth,
half asleep, waits to be fed.

Outlived by Time

The empty hearse skimmed away
like a dead leaf chased by the wind,
pallbearers slipped off to their offices,
the church basement breathed
fresh coffee and stale odors,
he overlooked the grief masks of the
inheritors while he shook their hands.
He felt no worm of mortality webbing
his eighty-five-year-old face, only pain
from this latest wound.
His cane like a scythe whacked off
dandelion heads as he walked home,
the rewards of a walk home, home, home,
a shell to keep out strangers and the rain.
Pools of eyes under white-haired cliffs
reflected the shadows he shaped in words,
"Damn," he said softly, "every time
I see one of my friends, he's dead."

The Visitor

In the heat of the afternoon
I stopped for a drink and while
my sweat dried and hands relaxed
looked at my work. The corn showed
nary a weed, the plants dark green,
the third leaf showing, sun wakened,
a meadowlark bobbed on a fence post
and pumped out a trickle of song,
a morning glory climbed the gate post
I leaned against and barbed wire
ran shining along the field's edge
to protect my ownership.
A breath of air touched me softly
like a bird's wing across my face

and suddenly I felt like a stranger
who stayed here only by the sufferance
of growing things and I almost bowed
to the earth as a favored guest might
who was invited to stay out his visit.

A Return to Facts

You check out the office
for the last time, lock the door,
turn in the key and you and your
battered briefcase, two old companions,
follow the stairs and down the hall
filled with years of your steps.
You bleed a little, feel empty days
open ahead, feel somehow betrayed
by the clock tick you never thought
to hear. Strange, how the future
shrinks to a row of yesterdays.
The hell with them, let them mould
their way into history—old clothes
in a ragbag. The garden metaphor
seems foolish against real earth
when you work the seedbed with
your own hands. The hoe and rake
may be more enduring friends than
the ink-fed knives carving theses
into academic shape. Now on the camp stool
you reserve for holidays, sit and watch
the real thing, the actual sprouting seed
form green rows and climbing vines.
This is a way back to your beginnings,
cultivate a field of facts until
words fall away like dry pods.

1976

Forked Road

It's hard to decide sometimes
whether to stay or go, to face
driving snow or stay by a warm fire.
But if you don't go, the little
sharp teeth of what you ought to do
will gnaw at your comfort until
you find fault with your dinner
and don't sleep well that night.
Even a small duty will give you
a hard time if you don't listen.
I know a farmer who turned his horses
out to pasture before he locked
the barn doors to prove he could
make up his mind without a nudge
from an old copybook. It's what
you learn from experience that teaches
you how to face a forked road.
I heard a forecast this morning that said,
"Showers and thunderstorms, otherwise
mostly clear."—Hard to beat that
for coming to grips with the weather
either inside or out.

Veterans' Day

How thankful they should be,
the young men I know,
playing their games, excited by girls,
muscle in their language,
voices uneven as their beards.
Thunder on the horizon
breeds no fear in them, hand curved
to catch and throw, to clasp
books, shoulders, breasts,
never the chill steel of bayonet,
nor slimy vines, nor ooze of jungles,
beds in mud, blankets of snow.
How thankful, ears tuned to bellowing
transistors, shrieks and laughter,
teachers' assignments, coaches' bark,
not captain's command, nor sergeant's shout,
nor machine guns' clatter, nor the
stealthy step in the dark.
How thankful, their names scribbled
on papers, letters, walls, sign-ups,
not written in stone on a statue
in the town square where pigeons roost
and no one reads them. How thankful,
November 11 is just another day off
when bells and whistles sound at eleven a.m.

They died, goddam it, they died,
the young men for whom the bells toll,
never to have homes, or wives or children,
or the comfort of a warm bed.

Self-Portrait

The mirror lacks depth,
lacks the signature of mercy,
shows me a naked face, long, big ears,
narrow eyes, features unnoticed
by the inner eye. I am what I am
to the reflection. Break the glass
and behind it a bottle of aspirin.
Who said, "I have traveled widely
in Concord?" My tracks aren't meant
to be followed. I shadow the landscape
of mind with landmarks and forget them.
My roots don't show. Cut down a tree
to count the rings, my stump would be
different. A swollen seed, hatching egg,
a heifer dropping her first calf,
the pain of something broken, life draws
a first breath—I have seen it.
As I look into the glass, no vision
shines out, no stoic spirit, no halo
above gray hair, deep wrinkles,
scarred forehead, I cannot find myself here.
I lean toward tomorrow, a bricklayer
without bricks, a newsboy trying to collect,
an old farmer with empty pockets
impatient for a new year.

Frustrations

Thoughts run like mice
in the pantry and if I
catch one the trap squeezes out
eyes and dung. I save the bait
and throw away the body—what use
is a dead thought to a man
whose house won't keep out
mice that aren't thoughts
and whose head can't keep in
thoughts that aren't mice?

66

Harvest Claim

The clover field in bloom seemed innocent
of any appetite except the urge to bloom
which loosed and fatted blossoms in the sun
as if there were no other months than June,
no other shade than purple, no response
but drift in waves under the wind's light hand
while bumblebees wrung honey from the land.

But I was sobered when the autumn rains
beat the earth to its bones and drove the roots
into their tunnels to hide what they could keep
of the bags of summer sap; the harvest plains
echo to sounds of metal and I weep
for the fields of summer lost and the end of play.
The crop, once sown, must learn what the sickles say.

Landscape—Iowa

No one who lives here
knows how to tell the stranger
what it's like, the land I mean,
farms all gently rolling,
squared off by roads and fences,
creased by streams, stubbled with groves,
a land not known by mountain's height
or tides of either ocean.
a land in its working clothes,
sweaty with dew, thick-skinned loam,
a match for the men who work it,
breathes dust and pollen, wears furrows
and meadows, endures drought and flood.
Muscles swell and bulge in horizons
of corn, lakes of purple alfalfa,
a land drunk on spring promises,
half-crazed with growth—I can no more
tell the secrets of its dark depths
than I can count the banners in a
farmer's eye at spring planting.

Dirge for an Old Wound

Any root worth its salt
tries to stay alive in spite of
stony ground, drought or lack
of sun, the push for growth
wakes a need that takes what
nourishment it can with greedy mouth.
Notice how gnarled, twisted,
turned back on itself a root can be
and yet deliver the goods.
I've seen a tree cut by an ax,
marred by a fence, rubbed raw
by an animal, bleed while its roots
pumped up sap to break out leaves
in their usual glory so birds
could sing in its green house.
It still stood against the wind.
If too much attention to pain
neglects the morning of a new day,
better let the inner man bleed
than bind up an old wound when
there is work to be done.

Virgin Prairie

This old squaw of a prairie
with no fence or furrow wrinkles
squats by a country cemetery
under the shelter of a lost deed.
She wraps herself in a blanket
of buffalo grass, beaded with
shooting stars, sweet alyssum,
fringed gentians, tiny yellow and
lavender petals, with wild roses
tangled in vines. She dreams
the memory of a wigwam empty now
save ashes whose breath rises
in ghost smoke of the past.

At Least on the Surface

People who live in neighborhoods
learn how to tell "How are you?" from
"What do you want?" without a committee
report. This keeps us in good standing
with ourselves and with each other
at least on the surface where soft words
sometimes mask hard thoughts like,
"The son-of-a-bitch mows his lawn early
every Sunday morning!" We keep our hedges
trimmed, steps repaired, houses painted,
practice collective complaints over the
city's negligence in gathering dead leaves,
removing snow, fixing pavements, cracking down
on noisy cars and motorcycles. There is a
sprinkling of churchgoers, earnest souls,
a raft of parents hung-up on the PTA.
The kids play both ends against the middle
by wearing Sunday School faces while they
sneak out to "learn about life." Eighth-grade
girls scamper out of sight, then stop and
light cigarettes, puffing and strutting with
the awkwardness known only by teen-agers.
See? On the surface everything well-kept,
conscience-clean, paid-up, sunny-skies, all
respectable as a chrome-plated, plush-lined,
tinted-glass automobile, the kind we buy and drive.
But dark currents run underneath, rain keeps
the hay from being made, lightning strikes
and blinds don't always cover windows.

What Wind

crept in to slam the door
when you went out, to thrust
an elbow in the kitchen's face,
open the cupboard door to black
my eye, and leave me with spilled
coffee to remember you by?

University

Morning light throws a wreath
over the buildings, wakes the clock tower,
mist lies on the grass, a butterfly
waits for the sun to dry its wings,
the sky's pages shine with color,
too high for a message from liberal arts.

The janitor shakes his mop
from a third-floor window, no one
hears the echoes of last night's music,
the silence rips like a silk cloth
when a cardinal by the graduate school
whistles and repeats.

A flag joins the top of the flagpole,
doors swing open, feet sound in the halls,
a student turns the key of his locker
and takes out a briefcase so lightweight
it might contain his future
and waits for the bell.

Outside summer dances with leaves,
midges swarm, balloons of dreams
rise unchecked to bump against the sky.

Valley and Mountain

The valley floor crawls with streets
and utters the sound of traffic,
I talk to myself to hear a human voice,
the mountain waits with its wisdom.
My daily path from square to square
traps me in the facts of footsteps
while the day's meaning seems to ride
like a hawk, small and soaring,
over the mountain's silence.

Stream and Tree

The stream's promise
of an easy bed could lull
a troubled man to sleep.
No dismay would alarm
the pastures nearby,
horses would still graze,
jays screech from a dying elm,
grasshoppers snap into
the depth of afternoon,
bluebottle flies attend
a dead rabbit.
But the young oak I lean against
grips earth firmly, reaches
toward the sun, grows into its future.
It makes my thoughts root deep
as I nod to the horses,
whistle at the jays,
drink from the stream and try
to think enough green signs
so I can go it alone.

The Blame

It is difficult to explain
yourself to a woman who is
explaining herself to you
after you have both agreed
the affair has petered out
and you try to excuse each
other from the blame you feel
you each deserve. The words
cluster around your mouths
like a flock of birds on a
telephone wire that sits there
momently, then flies away
leaving the perch empty but
the wire alive with its
throbbing tongues.

71

Spring Fever

Sun touched I sit on a
frail box beside the garden
tools waiting for the noon
whistle.

All around me spring sweats
in labor, I hear roots push
in deep tunnels, stir in a
bird's egg, smell dew on a
thrust of buds, feel thorns
of a climbing rose.

How many springs lie piled in
the cellar of my mind, in baskets
of unplanted bulbs, dried seeds,
a litter of odds and ends of
withered trials? Now spring shines
again from green wisteria vines.

Sun touched I sprawl in slow motion
on honeysuckle clouds, deaf to the
growl of accusing bees.

Don't Ask the Professor

Don't bring any more naked questions
for me to clothe with answers.
Styles change too fast to keep up with
and I'm going out of business.
For one thing, I can't get material
I can depend on, it's shoddy, shrinks
when wet, won't hold a press. It's hard
to match with thread, seams gap,
alterations show, bias ravels,
an uneven weave spoils the pattern. . . .
Perhaps my eye isn't what it was,

the scissors don't cut true along
the chalk line, when I pin pieces
together the shape won't hold and
the pins fall out. I say the situation
is out of hand and you better try
ready-made styles. I'm tired of trying
to please customers who don't want
my kind of truth anymore, let them shop
for answers in some other place.

Pressed Flowers

The flowers we picked last summer
and pressed in your ladies magazine
have crumbled to dry blossoms
and feed a winter fire. But they
remind me how you walked in sunlight,
red clovers in your hand, laughing,
while time turned cartwheels and
on a single spike of timothy
two bobolinks fluttered together.

Potencies

Earth, sun-plowed, rain-swept, trembles
at seed stir, thrust of root and foot,
summer sweats in birth and growth,
I in overalls as judge's robes sentence
tares from wheat, weevils from bins,
rats from stored boxes but the
judgment word is never final. Behind
my back I know a thistle fouls the
lily bed, a quick tail whisks beneath
the cellar wall, on some clear nights
a ring frames the moon.

Father

Nailheads broke off with the sound
of rifle shots, blizzard winds
shook the house, snug as squirrels
we burrowed in our quilts
until morning came.

The upstairs an arctic cave,
a floor of ice, but father
braved it and we heard him downstairs
shake the hard-coal stove
until all its isinglass eyes
glowed red, the low roar
of a bucket of coal poured
in its mouth.

When he called, "You can come now,"
we scuttled downstairs to dress
in the lovely warmth.

But no one ever said, thank you,
or praised him, or simply,
we love you.

Wren Logic

The stump braces its roots,
bumps off ax and spade,
shows no sign of giving up
before I do. I stop for breath,
watch two wrens build a nest in a
box hung in a tree. They poke sticks
through its round door and after
each success they flutter their wings
and sing their heads off. Plainly
all's well until they hoist a forked
twig too wide for the door. They turn

it over and over and end for end
as if a change in circumstances would
alter the situation. I smile in spite
of my blisters, knowing well the law
of facts, when suddenly the stick
goes in and I am left without a leg
to stand on before this miracle of
wren logic.

Day after Day

The baby cries in its crib,
the young mother gives it
her startled glance to play with,
the father fingers his new moustaches,
packs anxieties in his briefcase,
holds up a finger for the wind,
sails to his office.
Beer in the icebox keeps better
than dollar bills, the rent wakes
and stares at the calendar,
a grocery list says the clock is fast,
why the hell wear out shoes
if no one smiles after the dance?
Who would die to be born again,
happiness stays in its mousehole,
the traps are all baited with despair—
a bottle of whiskey to take to church,
the sacred wafer to bribe the bar girls.

Revival

The anxious hours numb me
but day's clock counts a low
November sun still warm at noon,
fields with the smell of damp decay,
a hawk fetters mice to their furrows,
wind bends the stiff weeds. I write
the record on odds and ends of mind,
shaken by leaf-fall I would have
tramped through in happier years.
Now in a whirl of dry grass I read
the signs that end love, but the sun
throws its web over my face, blinds me
to shadows, and I see how wind speaks
in bare trees, the hawk lives his way
in the sky, mice stuff their burrows
with seeds, a man reads autumn's words
like a text for his thought and remembers
the sharp taste of salt on his tongue.

Winter Mood

Warm in mackinaw and boots I read
the morning's message on my land,
on frosty vines dead leaves post
news of the sap's descent, a mouse
scribbles in snow on the stump
of a fallen elm, a mile away a phrase
of smoke invokes a house, my breath
repeats itself in adjectives, and
flashing wings refute the stare
of vacant places, rabbit tracks define
the fence row where a crow
in three sharp jeers mocks
my signature on the field's page.

1977

Growing Up

It is time to leave the grove,
the warm dark secret embrace of trees,
the wigwam of horseblankets and
maple poles, the campfires where we ate
half baked potatoes and charred sweetcorn.
The years have straddled our backs
and spurred us into the open sky beyond
the forest paths we travelled
to a field alive with its sowing.
This is the temple of work marked by
the stations of sweat and callouses.
Now the dung loader and tractor's voice
will send anniversary greetings
to our knees and shoulders, and a
mouldy saddle and rusty bit offer
proof of our fleet footed pony.
Come out of the woods, the snakes
chuckle in the gardens, long windows
of the mind look out on auction sales
flying their pennants along the tired
main street of property.

Flight and Return

The locked house next door
now shows signs of life,
people have moved in,
a man and his wife.

Don't let the word spread,
please keep the kids quiet,
don't question the mailman,
folks might start a riot

if a few of them knew
they had come back again
to a place no one thought
would be occupied when

the owners moved out,
sold the place for a song,
pulled shades down for grief,
for right turned to wrong,

as the floors of a heart
cave in under the weight
of stone words piled up
by the white hands of hate.

Calendar's Mischief

A day of shock,
sharp sense of loss
in the withered berry,
shrunken vine and grass
stiff with frost.
Now fireweed blooms,
pebbles gleam in creeks,
the trees astound me,
I have not worn such color
even in my thoughts.
The slant sun blazes
on a window, green bleeds

from the garden stems,
clouds peer from the horizon
as wind wraps the house
and moans down the chimney.
And I see, with limited view,
how a man on his threshold
feels betrayed by mischief
in his calendar.

Lock the Door

Now you have burned the letters—
did you save one?—no, no, let them all go.
The afternoon drifts into twilight,
the peace of evening shadows the silence
of an empty house where emptiness
drains your eyes of tears,
if you could still weep.
You are no priest with holy water
to wash the past from your hands,
revive the dead plant in its dry earth
hanging by the window, nor wipe
the dust from the tables once altars
for fresh flowers.
Do you sweat to restore your pictures,
or do you sweat here to prove the owner
will not let his books mold,
the dresses hang for strangers to discard?
You walk the floor to make a sound
to keep you company, wipe down spider webs
as if the years lay in wait to trap you
in the snare of your own spinning.
Flies lie here that have forgotten flight,
the fireplace sits in its ashes,
no scouring powder under the sink
to scrub the stains from the linoleum,
you lock the door when you go out
burdened by the calendar.
There is no sorrow as desperate
as the memory of happy days
when you are sick, old and alone.

The Way It Is

Prepare the ground, I told her,
channel a straight row, select
the seeds, drop them in the
open furrow, and cover them.
Observe these facts, I said, to keep
a garden from being helter skelter.
A radish seed won't become a turnip
because it's in a turnip row.
Seeds carry instructions,
even know the season, look how corn
sweats and heats at planting time.
(Lectures in her ears,
a mosquito buzz in bed.)

Why tug nature's skirts, she asked?
Let things grow their own way,
all this digging and raking and
pulling a string tight just to make
a straight row—does a radish care?
Why not crooked rows, room for more
seeds? Look at you pulling weeds,
don't weeds have rights, aren't they
alive with a will to grow?

I chopped angrily, hoed out
a young cabbage plant, left
a thistle standing.

Who? Who?

Do you ever stop to wonder—
say, right now, this morning—
what you'd see in the mirror
with your mask off?
Oh, I don't mean casual glimpses
when you are shaving,
or combing your hair,
or cleaning out blackheads,

when you hardly see anybody at all.
Nor when you play a role,
a time when you are jealous
and thoughts about the girl
cut like fine wires and your face snarls,
or maybe at a party you took
one drink too many and made
an ass of yourself and you can see
the shamed look in the eyes all right.
No, I mean eyeball to eyeball,
you look that guy in the mirror
right in the face without any coverup
and, my god, he's a stranger,
someone you never saw before.
A face drowned in a pool of glass
floats gently on the surface
caught in the drifting weeds of time,
mute in the shadow of my question,
Who, who are you?

Same Thing but Different

The paper boy slammed the screen door
as he always does two jumps ahead
of my alarm clock and gets me up to
wash my face, shave and dress. Then
the mailman banged the lid of the
mailbox as he does each day, and the
garbage men tossed the lids of the
cans on the ground the way they do,
and the meter man whistled his way
down the basement steps always
off key. And I prodded with surprise
into the belly of my thoughts
to ask how this routine could replay
itself so casually as if your absence
didn't matter and damned if I didn't
burn the toast and let the coffee pot
boil over explaining this rip-off
to my conscience.

Whatever Happened

When I was young I discovered
a new country inhabited by folk
who lived for my fear and pleasure
in an acorn cup or castle of cloud
or asleep behind a wall of roses.
I walked the paths of Sherwood Forest
or sank underground where a gnomelike smith
forged a sword and I killed the dragon.
I became a prince, then a giant,
I snatched Excalibur from the white hand
of the Lady of the Lake, sat at the
Round Table, rescued my mother from
a witch's spell, put her in charge
of the King and his men and lived in
the whoop and glory of my own world.

Now on a street of dying elms I puzzle
over the dull prose style of work and worry.
Where did the magic go, the wonder
that armed me with my power each morning,
let me revenge my tears and punishments.
What flip of calendar leaves brought me
to this bowlegged street, this boxlike house,
this mirror where I see an endless stretch
of suburbs, lawns, houses, meetings,
parties, PTA, Rotary Club, golf at four,
bridge at eight, who knows the time.
I let the princess die, the giant win,
the wizard destroy the castle, the witch
survive to eat the children, I forgot the way
to Sherwood Forest, have never kept my vow
to kill the wolf, find the foot to fit
the slipper. I am charged by myself
with murder, wear dark glasses, wear gloves,
false teeth, paid off with a sports car,
swimming pool, tax exempts, stylish wife,
a butt for statistics, gelded by habits,
indicted and condemned by the voice
of facts.

Susanna and the Elders

Let us put thought aside
and imagine a pool
clear, water smooth as the
cheek of a still moment.
Hide it in a nest of fern fronds
above the grass, beneath the trees.
What balance, delicate,
quiet as a caught breath,
sustains interlaced images
grown used to each other.
Now stir the depths and produce
the shape of a girl, she wears
the air of innocent youth,
nude of course (please do not
escape into fantasy, we have
more work to do), she worships
the secret soul of the place,
the tension tightens but her nakedness
keeps the harmony unbroken.
She smiles at herself, then
shatters the mirror with her foot,
joins the pool up to her breasts.
Shadows hold their breath,
trees, flowers, ferns and water
wait for the spirit to speak
and with its silence become a
garland in the ritual of the unexplored.
(Now comes the bad part.) Like trumpets
of triumph the brassy eyes of the Elders
tumble the walls of privacy and a
startled gasp erects no shelter.
Communion bread molds, wine sours,
innocence finds no wilderness
safe from barbarians' hands.

Eighty Birthdays

This cake, a snow topped hill,
bare, not eighty candles to march
with flaming banners as a victory
over time. No, the decorator
with his spurting artery stained
a red eighty against the white.
If I could blow out eighty candles
and make a wish, I would wish
for a new body, strong as a tree trunk,
hungry for love as a stallion
searching the meadow for thighs
hidden in the grass.
I ride this old donkey,
a trembling beast, lame footed,
worn teeth, blind to directions. . . .
He still haunts me, my stranger,
the sturdy footed memory
with the ape still in his heart
who strayed through the country
gathering grapes and girls' cries,
kin to the dawn man who gnawed bones
and painted trophies
on his cave's wall.

Hostility to Order

Today the sun's eye
curls green leaves,
stares me down, earth
under my steps cracks
in dry protest. What?
A conspiracy? I am no
outcast, leper, pariah
knocking at the gates.
I own my homestead and
work it to impose discipline,
straight rows, weedless fields.
I take my stand here and now
to ripen seeds into harvest.

I do not cringe from the sun's
glare nor earth's apostacy.
But the still rooms, empty
doorway, the loneliness,
(after you left on your long journey),
persuades me again of the hostility
to order in my world.

Not Born Again

This land partly from me,
given back all the years
of my slow death where I
discarded skin after skin,
layers of growth sloughed off
to make earth, I shed myself here.

Here fingernails I pared,
there an old jacket in shreds,
a rubber boot left in a tile ditch,
a notebook on calving time
dissolving in manure, a straw hat
blown off in a field, and everywhere
drops of sweat, pee beside the
corner post—all part of me
going back to make land and grow
whatever will grow. Immortality?
Who said Immortality?
Nothing like me in the morning glory bell,
thistles resemble nothing in me,
foxtail and smartweeds sport no features
of mine—my crops? They grow
the way I plant them.
Something of me goes back to earth
in a stream of ashes burned
from my life until I blow away
like a dried leaf yet with no features
for a wild rose to copy.

Words that Smell Bad

Neighbor, your "friendly" note arrived
via the mailman and I wondered if we
weren't speaking or if you had bronchitis.
I am with you in keeping trim yards
and a clean alley. I will prune the
tree limb that overhangs your line,
pick up the beer cans from the picnic table,
level the pile of dirt where I dug out
the elm stump. If you will clean your
Sunday papers out of my hedge, shore up
your wall spilling on my lawn, collect
the turds from the hound you loose
after dark to run through my back yard.
Let us define our views on cleanliness
and order, we Americans have a knack for
instructing our neighbors. We who live
with polluted water, smog, junkyards and
the detritus from a people who litter
streets with their crap and all the poop
that squirts from our bottles of amusement.
Sure, we say, clean, clean up, clean up the
blacks, the colleges, the U.N., Cuba, the
whole caboodle, the world needs our deodorant.
Once a game warden sniffed around my father
for a pheasant shot out of season and my father
said, "Take your nose out of my ass."
Neighbor, I wish I had thought of that.

Mother

The photograph fades, turns yellow,
but the woman still sits erect
on a velvet chair, her piled hair
adorned with combs, her bodice tight and smooth,
sleeves in folds, her skirt billows,
one child at her feet, one beside her—
she is beautiful.

86

If time shadowed her proud smile
with workworn hands, tremulous mouth,
the fierce hawks in her eyes
sent him howling like a beaten dog.
Her children remember the odor
of home baked bread, a table bright
with silver, white with linen
where the farm rubbed its elbows,
numb fingers hanging out sheets
in freezing weather, young and hungry minds
fed with books and magazines from
her saved chicken money. She bent
like a tree in the wind, scarred by
wounds of love and labor.
But now in the picture she lifts
her beautiful proud head, innocent
of praise, of tears, or stormclouds
threatening the sky at sunset.

The Will to Possess

Shoemaker had some Bokhara seed to sell,
the neighbors hurried to buy, filled with hope.
You'd think the seed had been blessed by the Pope,
how the word got out, none of us would tell.

Rumor whispered, here was a special seed.
I guess it's natural we keep looking for
a bigger crop than we've ever had before.
Rain lurks in every cloud when you're in need.

But still we didn't know what the seed would grow,
the hint and secrecy just tempted us that day.
What we could count on Shoemaker wouldn't say;
here was his price and here was the seed to sow.

In spite of this we felt the urge to buy
this gold-husked seed, strange, with a foreign name
(knowing that hope and harvest are not the same)
we couldn't resist the gamble. We had to buy.

Facts

I do not read portents,
bars of sunlight through a cloud,
a dog howling at night,
a bridge washed out,
a crow perched on a dead limb—
let some reader of oracles
interpret the signs.
I read on the day's work sheet
the facts of my existence,
corn to grind, pens to clean,
teach a calf to suck,
wrap roses for winter.
The wind rustles dead stalks,
says nothing I don't know,
my labor tongued hands assure me
that my sky is not falling
in spite of sickness, weather and age.

I Set My Chair

I set my chair on the driveway
and try to feel my way
into the evening solitude
as the sun and wind both call
it a day and walk over the hill.
I want a drink from the well
of silence, I want to feel
the green hand of twilight
full of its own quiet
touch my face.
Just merge, I said to myself,
into this country of stillness
as if you were a tree or wave of grass
where no one shouts or starts machines.
But the mood did not come at my call
and all I did was to strike at a swarm
of gnats around my head and swear
at a kid on a motorcycle

who had left its muffler at home.
I watch as the twilight without
a murmur frees the sky of light,
I shed a coat of hot summer sun
and shawl myself in silence.
Not quite, the motorcycle spurts
a smoke ring of obscenities—
the vulgarity of the young
is beyond apology—so I lean back
and rest my head on the stillness,
absorbed by the holy calm
as the day dries its sweat and
shuts the door. Here, so still
the air seems to hold its breath,
is a transcendence of natural things
I cannot imitate. Wrapped in the folds
of my efforts, held in the hollow
of a tree's shadow, my head buzzes
with a swarm of thoughts like gnats
as if a hole had been torn in
my screen of meditation.

Born Each Morning

What a shocking way to enter the world,
whacked on the back by a stranger,
held up naked by the heels
in front of strange women,
inspected like some plucked chicken.
But each morning I feel the exposure
when I slide from the warm and cozy
amniotic atmosphere of the bed
where all night I floated in a
suspension of sleep. Now like a yell
of beginning, the sharp glare of light,
the demand on arms and legs after night's
languor, groping through morning chores
when all still seems obscure in
the cloudy terminals of night. What carrot
leads the poor donkey from his stall
each morning, the dim image in the mirror
that brays his protest for his rebirth each day.

Vacation in Colorado

The street's hullaballoo tramps
through the morning with an armful
of tradition faded by motel signs.
He hoisted a backpack and fled
to the mountain. The stream ran clear,
a Stellar's jay jeered, aspen leaves
whirled, rocks gripped his shoes,
the sun burned off the fog—too
burned off clouds back of his eyes.

His glance circled, wilderness paths
offered directions but a flag of smoke
led him like a compass needle.
When he broke through the underbrush
he stared at the town dump, burning trash,
old mattresses, piles of papers, tin cans.
His eyes closed over the bright image
of a solitary campfire on a rocky ledge
blanketed with pink columbine.

Ute Cemetery

Gravestones lean every which way,
some, uprooted, lie flat. Grass
contests with weeds, the fence of
split rails unmakes itself
where the posts rot. A clump of
fireweed blazes beside stalks of
lupine as if neglect could not
erase all memorials. One wooden slab
says, "Soldier, 25th Infantry,
Illinois." Death does not need
his name. All the Indians lie heaped
under a long mound, not even marked
"Warrior." Here passion sleeps
in the graves. The yells and cries,

the hot bullets of Meeker Flats
awake no echoes, rouse no memories,
speak only from yellow pages
of an old newspaper. Life became
death with no meaning for today's
tourist. No one remembers the bitter
struggle, the lost cause, the bravery
in victory and defeat. No one even
remembers the cemetery.

It Never Went Away

In daytime the cellar seemed safe,
whatever hid there, slept, or rested
or changed shape. The jars sat primly
on shelves, potato bin and apple barrel
breathed their odors, a mouse trap
guarded a corner, a smoked ham hung
from a beam, all friendly, at your service.
But at night it came out. Even armed
with a lantern you could hear it, a sigh,
scrape of claws, sudden shadow on the wall,
a slight hiss through bared teeth.
You climbed the stairs backward, lantern
held in front, daring it to come, afraid
to turn your back. Upstairs you were thankful
to be rescued. It still lay in wait, even when
you grew up and were ashamed to tell it.
You, late night comer, braced your foot
against the garage and fled for your life
to the back door, thankful for Carlo's bark,
a chance to dry your sweat.

A man woke from a troubled dream, got up
turned on all the lights, searched the house.
Stepped outside, fired his shotgun twice
into the darkness to say who is master here.

91

The Enemy

That girl who now switches
her tail, juts her breasts,
struts her wares, is scared in
her blood as a rabbit that knows
the hawk waits. All that flesh
in bloom for the summer, the
withering touch of her calendar
still hidden. Silently she begs
in her need for the lustful eye
to seize her in its talons, for
the gardener's hand to pluck her
while her perfume lasts. She denies
the grinning skull behind her cheeks,
a skeleton's bones in those long
brown, lascivious legs, those soft
embracing arms. Yet she knows
the ambush where her enemy lurks,
and her lips open in a laugh
shaped like a shriek of terror.

Too Many Defeats Dull the Spirit

The worst was
too damn much rain,
the corn opening its first leaf,
the beans just breaking through—
you know a beanstalk
arches its back to open
the crust of ground and pulls
the leaves through after it.
Rain washed the earth down
like a silt glacier and
covered everything, smothered it,
killed it.
I had only a couple of low corners
but Henry Jensen lost all his bottom land.
He replanted twice, too late for corn
and still the beans could hardly

break through. It gave Henry
a kind of emotional seizure and
he stayed inside his house for a week.
His wife said he spent all his time
sitting in the bedroom under an umbrella,
but you have to allow for a woman
planting some ornamental borders
around the plain truth.

Cleaning the Barn

We put it off, not having to prove
we were Hercules, but the day came
(as it always does with work not done)
when we took our forks, spit on our hands,
hung our coats on a nail and started.
All winter the calves tramped straw bedding
to hard packed manure with a yellow smell,
tied in with straw and two feet thick,
every forkful strained our shoulders,
with every forkful we grew thick grass
on meadows where we spread this waste
from the farm's gut, remains of corn and hay
back to the fields again. It was a place
of odors, incense to bless the land,
we tugged, pulled, swore, joked,
stained with sweat and our slippery loads,
dregs of harvest for another harvest.
A spring day on the wheel of seasons.
When the pen was clean we smelled to high heaven,
lame in our muscles, weary beyond rest,
we picked up our coats, banged the forks
into their racks, made our bed on a
bale of hay, heard for applause
a banging barn door.

Judgment by Spring Rain

Some snarl faced poet
in his weedy, unfenced youth,
booted age into the winter season.
Would that age had the energy
of a blizzard or the bite of zero
or even the sculptured thoughts
lying in cold patterns on drifted snow.
Watch for the thirst for change
when a March sun gets a real foothold
in the sky and melts the drifts.
Patches of ground widen under trees,
see the debris that rides up,
a broken-backed board,
a double faded newspaper with
who knows what headlines, junk from
the past—these show an aged mind
at its worst.
A spring rain will swell roots,
make them bulge with a sprout
or bloat in decay.

Each to Its Own Purpose

They said, don't use words
like epistemology in a poem,
use short, fat, beetle-browed
Anglo-Saxon words with
big butts, thick shoulders,
that clutch, hump, sweat, sleep,
that plant, grow, reap, store,
shake, fear, starve, haunt, die.
Epistemology, they said, in a poem
is like using a castrated bull
to settle your cows.
But I don't buy that, why castrate,
let him do what he was born to do.

94

It seems to me there's confusion here
between the use of a sieve and a bucket,
do you want to carry water or strain out pulp?
It's the joy of knowing that makes
the facts shine, or the Wise Men
would never have made their long trip,
nor any of us found our way
out of the dark wood where
we were lost.

Shaped by Names

You must exist somewhere
back of the trellis of the names
I give you. I keep flinging
words like blossoms over the
lattice to fill the emptiness
if you are not there.

My tongue spells out syllables
like nets to catch you where
you drift on time's stream
that flows away from me. I search
for sounds that form a name
to bring you into the light.

I chant a rune that should
return you to the human shape
I knew, I ask you to appear.
If you are not my names for you
I am not who I was, I have
no place to go, my tongue knotted with silence.

Alive and Well

Don't fill the kitchen pot
with husks and nutshells,
nor wear the gunny sack of
poverty of spirit, nor cut
paper dolls from the daily press
to prove you are upset.
Cold and snow may bury the yard
with sleeping drifts but this
won't starve the cocky sparrows.
Days tick off on the season's
slow clock but we tell time by
an evening's fire and the door
we opened for a starving kitten
on a naked afternoon. There may be
a lesson in the endurance of roots
but let us be thankful
their long sleep is not our habit.

End of the Game
(FOR MY BROTHER ROBERT RUSSELL HEARST)

Two little boys dusty with pollen
would need clean faces to come
to the supper table. In the
cornfield we hid from each other,
racing up and down the rows like
rabbits, you always gave yourself
away with a snort of laughter.

It is your turn to hide while
I cover my eyes. I hear the rustle
and murmur of leaves drying in
the warm October sun. But now you
are quiet and I cannot find you.
Come out, brother, come out,
I am afraid. Soon it will be dark
and mother will scold us if
we are late for supper.

1978

Women Shearing Men

The wind whistles a bawdy tune,
ears fill with spring's rapture,
men gnaw on the bones of their jobs
blinded by their long hair.
Clouds soft as marshmallows soaked with rain
sink in the vast wallows of the sky.
Women lugging big shears
roam the streets driving the men
before them. Soon the men find themselves
penned in on every side and the shearing begins.
The women squat and hold the men's necks
between their knees, the men cry out
when the shears nick their ears and tender scalps.

All the while flocks of blackbirds
swing free above new leaves, dogs
flash back and forth through alleys,
a squirrel leaps to a tree in sudden frenzy,
a tricycle pushed by the wind falls
off a porch.

The women take a coffee break, heat
their coffee with a blowtorch from a
plumber's van, beef it up with a dollop
of bourbon, run fingers through the
men's hair, jostle them to the ground,
while the men huddle in small groups,
hands over their crotches.
The men with naked heads stray about
like strangers who have lost their way,
miserable as sheep without a shepherd.

No More Chores

The old farmer nurses rheumatic joints
in a wheelchair beside the window.
He watches spring come
with all the fullness thereof,
his eyes dim with the smoke of the past.

Memory plows the years
where he planted his future,
he feels between thumb and finger
the earth's soft body, his inward eye
shines with banners of leaves
waving from cornstalks.
Each morning he wakes
from dreams of past harvests
roused by the cry of a cock pheasant
in a nearby field.

He stares as if the days ran backward
through a mirror, in the corner
a spider waits in her web.
He tastes dust in the wind,
feels stems grow in his fingers,
the distant yammer of a tractor
reminds him of hard calloused hands,
he smiles as he nods off to sleep.

Bereaved

Granted a meeting with her,
on the steps, in the hall, or a
room, granted too, an occasion,
return of a book, a business talk,
casual invitation, what occurred
seemed on the surface scarcely
worth mentioning. She made up
a smile, offhand greeting, an eddy
in the day's tide. But out of her words

welled tears, grief of eyes overflowing,
cheeks caught in the grimace of the
lonely of heart.
I told her there is the sudden break
called death, and the long suffering
called death, and we are not free
to choose, the end is the same.
Only you can speak for your lonely bed.
You cannot depend on us, the day comes
when you make your wailing wall private,
not to be seen by family or friends,
you keep your passion to yourself,
let the wound heal slowly.

But she was not comforted.

A Disowner

Not my world today
I find ghouls
in the graves of my ancestors,
jackals yapping over a lion's skin.
I live where the two-faced man,
the split tongue, mocking applause,
hiss of envy, poison smile,
owns the time.
It takes courage
to stand by your name when somewhere
a computer records your mis-steps,
spies on your bathroom recess.

The land keeps its promises
where even a barren field
brings a crop of weeds to harvest.
I find no duplicity in an ear of corn,
no moral decay in a brood sow,
I belong to furrows and fence rows.
I was not born to wear out my boots
chasing down a paved street
calling for a policeman.

Dragon Lesson

This country needs live dragons,
real fire breathing, tail swishing,
scaly, gold guarding, maiden snatching,
nasty tempered beasts. The real McCoy,
that would terrorize the countryside,
eat a few defiant people, burn down
churches that don't believe in dragons,
not fake scenes on a stupid TV screen.
Think how we would huddle together,
crying out for another St. George, and
longing for peace. Think of us longing for,
pleading for, praying for peace, just
imagine it. And think of the lesson our
brave young men would learn, that if they
win the gold they have to keep the girl.

The Inevitable Words like Sign Posts

This morning's paper carried a story
that stabbed me in the soft underbelly
of memory where I am most vulnerable.
Another old friend had left the field
and closed the gate behind him.

I walk back along the road until
those nights appear when we played
poker, drank prohibition booze and
harangued like pitchmen at a county fair.
*Mac Kantor   Don Murphy   Cliff Millen
Stuffy Walters   Viggo Justesen*
names from the great days.

Now in my thoughts I hold a quiet
service with the candles and altar
we knelt before hoping our prayers
reached the Surveyor who drew
the maps of our future. But in these days
only the inevitable words like sign posts
mark the way to the autumn woods
where leaves fall.